£5.00

GW00658613

Opening up
Ruth

JONATHAN PRIME

DayOne

Opening up
Ruth

JONATHAN PRIME

'Clear, insightful and compelling: Jonathan Prime opens up the book of Ruth, showing how it fits in the Bible, applies to us today and most of all, how God's kindness can change your life.'

Colin S. Smith,
Senior Pastor,
Arlington Heights Evangelical Free Church,
Arlington Heights, Illinois, USA

'The books in this series are known for their clarity and accessibility, yet with a rigour that belies their brevity. *Opening up Ruth* fits this bill exactly. Jonathan Prime's faithful handling of God's living Word brings out all its richness and relevance. Bible commentaries, whether short or long, often dull the inherent life of the Word; this one makes it live and sing! The further study notes and questions/discussion points at the end of each chapter would be excellent for personal devotions or for small group Bible study. And alongside a detailed technical commentary, as a preacher, I would definitely have this open on my desk. I trust my enthusiasm for Jonathan's work has come through in this review! I cannot commend it highly enough!

Robin Sydserff,
The Proclamation Trust

© Day One Publications 2007
First printed 2007

Unless otherwise indicated, Scripture quotations in this publication are from the Holy Bible: New International Version (NIV), copyright ©1973, 1978, 1984, International Bible Society.

ISBN: 978 1 84625 067 5

British Library Cataloguing in Publication Data available

Published by Day One Publications
Ryelands Road, Leominster, HR6 8NZ
Telephone 01568 613 740   FAX 01568 611 473

email—sales@dayone.co.uk
web site—www.dayone.co.uk
North American—e-mail-sales@dayonebookstore.com
North American web site—www.dayonebookstore.com

Designed by Steve Devane and printed by Gutenberg Press, Malta

To Mum and Sandra
Two women who have taken refuge
under the LORD's *wings*

List of Bible abbreviations

THE OLD TESTAMENT		1 Chr.	1 Chronicles	Dan.	Daniel
		2 Chr.	2 Chronicles	Hosea	Hosea
Gen.	Genesis	Ezra	Ezra	Joel	Joel
Exod.	Exodus	Neh.	Nehemiah	Amos	Amos
Lev.	Leviticus	Esth.	Esther	Obad.	Obadiah
Num.	Numbers	Job	Job	Jonah	Jonah
Deut.	Deuteronomy	Ps.	Psalms	Micah	Micah
Josh.	Joshua	Prov.	Proverbs	Nahum	Nahum
Judg.	Judges	Eccles.	Ecclesiastes	Hab.	Habakkuk
Ruth	Ruth	S.of.S.	Song of Solomon	Zeph.	Zephaniah
1 Sam.	1 Samuel	Isa.	Isaiah	Hag.	Haggai
2 Sam.	2 Samuel	Jer.	Jeremiah	Zech.	Zechariah
1 Kings	1 Kings	Lam.	Lamentations	Mal.	Malachi
2 Kings	2 Kings	Ezek.	Ezekiel		

THE NEW TESTAMENT		Gal.	Galatians	Heb.	Hebrews
		Eph.	Ephesians	James	James
Matt.	Matthew	Phil.	Philippians	1 Peter	1 Peter
Mark	Mark	Col.	Colossians	2 Peter	2 Peter
Luke	Luke	1 Thes.	1 Thessalonians	1 John	1 John
John	John	2 Thes.	2 Thessalonians	2 John	2 John
Acts	Acts	1 Tim.	1 Timothy	3 John	3 John
Rom.	Romans	2 Tim.	2 Timothy	Jude	Jude
1 Cor.	1 Corinthians	Titus	Titus	Rev.	Revelation
2 Cor.	2 Corinthians	Philem.	Philemon		

Introduction

The Bible is a library in one volume. Like a library it contains various types of literature. One type is story and Ruth is one of these. Ruth tells a true, simple, engaging and well-crafted story. It is a short story told in four chapters—eighty-five verses. Most importantly, it was written under the control and direction of God the Holy Spirit, and is part of God's transforming message for us.

Three New Testament passages give important clues as to how we should handle Old Testament books like Ruth:

1. Luke 24:27—'And beginning with Moses and all the Prophets, he explained to them what was said in all the Scriptures concerning himself.' Careful study of Ruth will help us to grow in our knowledge of the Lord Jesus Christ and to better understand his great purposes. To know the Lord Jesus better must be our aim in our study of any part of the Bible.

2. 1 Corinthians 10:11—'These things happened to them as examples and were written down as warnings for us, on whom the fulfilment of the ages has come.' Believers in the Lord Jesus Christ are the recipients of all the blessings God has promised to give the people he redeems. 1 Corinthians 10 refers to the experience of the Israelites in the desert, but the principle applies to all the events of the Old Testament. God not only caused the stories to be written

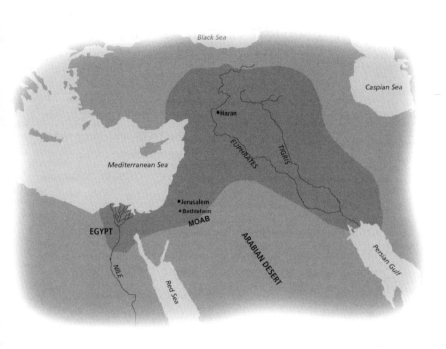

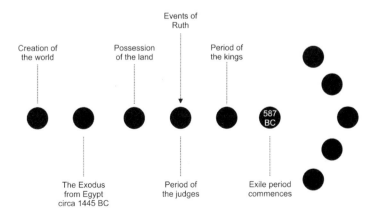

down for us, he caused them to happen for us. He caused the events recorded in Ruth to happen knowing that future generations would read the records of them and be taught by them. As we study Ruth we should not expect to be left unchanged.

3. Romans 15:4—'For everything that was written in the past was written to teach us, so that through endurance and the encouragement of the Scriptures we might have hope.' 'Endurance' implies difficulty. 'Encouragement' implies circumstances calling for courage. As Ruth teaches us about God's sovereign control of history and his transforming kindness to individuals, we should expect it to promote endurance and provide encouragement.

This short book is written with the purpose of *opening up* the Old Testament book of Ruth. It is designed to be read with the Bible *open* at Ruth. The greatest benefit will be obtained if its sections are read at the points suggested throughout this book.

Overview: God's transforming kindness

J. R. R. Tolkien's well-known epic *The Lord of the Rings* has three volumes: *The Fellowship of the Ring, The Two Towers* and *The Return of the King*. Imagine, however, reading only volume 2 (*The Two Towers*). Volume 2 tells a gripping tale. It is a good story on its own, but that is not how Tolkien meant it to be read. It is part of a much bigger story.

So it is with the Book of Ruth. It tells a great story, but it only makes complete sense when we discover how it fits with the bigger story of the whole Bible: the unfolding record of God's transforming kindness. Before reading this overview please read through the whole of Ruth. Reading it out loud takes about fifteen minutes. As you read, look out for the following:

REPEATED words or phrases
SURPRISES
EXPLANATIONS of events given by the narrator
EVIDENCES of the Lord taking action
MENTION of the word 'kindness'

REFERENCES to someone called a 'kinsman redeemer'
CONTRASTS between the beginning and end of the story

The Book of Ruth underlines three important and exciting truths:

Ruth is a story within the unfolding story of the Bible

The way a Bible book starts and ends often gives important clues as to its main message. Ruth 1:1 sets it in a particular time in the history of God's people, Israel: 'In the days when the judges ruled.' The days of the judges were dark days. The last verse of Judges explains why: 'In those days Israel had no king; everyone did as he saw fit.' If ever there was a recipe for disaster, that was it. The Book of Judges is a record of the chaos that occurs when people rebel against God and do their own thing.

Judges 2:10-3:6 describes the unhappy cycle of that time:

> **THE PEOPLE FORSOOK THE LORD**, the God of their fathers,
> who had brought them out of Egypt
> **THEY FOLLOWED AND WORSHIPPED VARIOUS GODS** of the
> peoples around them
> **PROVOKED TO ANGER**, the Lord sent enemies against them
> **THE PEOPLE** experienced great distress
> **IN THEIR DISTRESS**, the people cried out to the Lord
> **IN RESPONSE THE LORD RAISED UP JUDGES** (rescuing leaders),
> who saved them out of the hand of their enemies
> **WHEN THE JUDGE DIED**, the people returned to their rebellious
> ways, forsaking the Lord
> and so on …

The tragic cycle was repeated again and again, with each cycle plumbing greater depths than the one before. Read Judges 19 to 21: It is the record of the ungodly chaos that results when God's righteous rule is repeatedly ignored and everyone does as he or she sees fit. The implication of Judges 21:25 is that a king was needed to bring order to the chaos, which is where the story of Ruth comes in. It describes how the Lord acted to replace the chaos with order by providing his people with the king they needed. This is the message of the verses with which Ruth ends (4:18-22). The family line of Perez, to which Boaz, the husband of Ruth, belonged is recorded, ending with David, the son of Jesse. David was the king under whose rule the Lord's order was brought to the Lord's people (see 2 Sam. 8:15). In this way, Ruth is a story of the Lord's transforming kindness.

> The Book of Judges is a record of the chaos that occurs when people rebel against God and do their own thing.

One of the key words in Ruth is 'kindness' (e.g. 1:8; 2:20). It is a translation of the Hebrew word *hesed*, meaning 'loyal love'. It is the covenant love the Lord had committed himself to showing to his people. And the story of Ruth is the outworking of the Lord's kindness, as he sets in place the line into which the king his people need would be born. This shows Ruth's place in the unfolding story of the whole Bible. The last five verses of Ruth are also found in Matthew 1:3-6 in the genealogy of our Lord Jesus Christ. The Lord Jesus is declared to be the Lord's chosen King, descended from King David (and therefore from Boaz and

Ruth), who came as a result of the Lord's kindness to replace rebellious chaos with order.

Ruth is illustrative of the unfolding story of the Bible

Every detail of the plot has significance as it illustrates how the Lord fulfils his plan to show transforming kindness to rebellious people. As the story unfolds, three features of the way God works stand out:

God's control of circumstances

The story is told by a narrator who highlights how certain details 'just so happened' to fall into place. For example, chapter 2 starts with the information that Naomi had a relative on her husband's side from the clan of Elimelech, a man of standing, whose name was Boaz (2:1). When Ruth then goes out to glean in the fields, the narrator informs us: '*As it turned out*, she found herself working in a field belonging to Boaz, who was from the clan of Elimelech' (2:3). Bethlehem was a farming community. Fields belonged to various farmers. Ruth was a newcomer. She would not know whose field was whose. She did not know Boaz. Boaz did not know her. But the narrator wants us to know that God was in control of these details. It was no coincidence that Ruth ended up in Boaz's field. God doesn't do coincidences. Particular people are found in particular places at particular times and play their part in God's unfolding plan of transforming kindness.

God's use of apparently insignificant people

Ruth tells the story of very ordinary people. Naomi and Ruth are destitute widows. When they arrive in Bethlehem they possess nothing. In addition, Ruth is a foreigner; a Moabitess—from a nation with a scandalous pedigree and a bad history with Israel. But God did not use the rich and influential. He chose to use the lowly, unlikely and apparently insignificant.

God's provision of a redeemer

The words 'redeem/redemption/redeemer' occur twenty-three times in the eighty-five verses of Ruth. The essence of redemption is reversal—the reversal of a bad situation, at the expense of a redeemer. The situation of Naomi and Ruth was desperate. They discovered that Boaz was the perfectly suited kinsman-redeemer provided by God to reverse their fortunes.

These three features of the way God works are illustrative of the unfolding story of the whole Bible, which finds its fulfilment in God's transforming kindness through our Lord Jesus Christ. Was it a coincidence that the events of Ruth happened in Bethlehem where, 1000 or so years later, the Lord Jesus was to be born? Was it a coincidence that the Lord Jesus was born to an apparently insignificant young woman? (Note the similarity between Ruth 4:13 and Luke 2:7.) Was it a coincidence that, when the Lord Jesus was born, an elderly woman, called Anna, gave thanks to God and spoke to all who were looking forward to the *redemption* of Jerusalem (see Luke 2:38)?

> The essence of redemption is reversal—the reversal of a bad situation, at the expense of a redeemer.

Ruth is illustrative of the individual stories within the unfolding story

As the Lord's plan is fulfilled through Naomi and Ruth, we are provided with illustrations of the way individuals are transformed by his kindness. The Book of Ruth illustrates:

How the Lord transforms people caught up in the chaos of a rebellious world

That was Naomi's position at the start of the story. Caught up in the chaos caused by everyone doing as he or she saw fit, her life, once full, had become bitter and empty. Having lost her husband and her sons, and with no apparent hope of grandchildren, the future looked bleak. But then God acted in transforming kindness. The contrast between the Naomi we meet in 1:20-21 and in 4:14-17 is striking. Where there was death, the Lord brought new life. Where there was bitterness, the Lord brought joy. Where there was emptiness, the Lord brought fullness.

> As the Lord's plan is fulfilled through Naomi and Ruth, we are provided with illustrations of the way individuals are transformed by his kindness.

How the Lord's transforming kindness is experienced as refuge is taken under the shadow of his wings

Taking refuge in the shadow of the Lord's wings is a graphic picture of faith. It speaks of protection and security in time of trouble (see Psalm 36:7). According to 2:12, it was what Ruth had done by aligning herself with Naomi, Naomi's people and Naomi's God. It is a picture taken up by the Lord Jesus shortly before his death on the cross. To those who were refusing to submit to him as their King, he said, 'O Jerusalem, Jerusalem, you who kill the prophets and stone those sent to you, how often I have longed to gather your children together, as a hen gathers her chicks under her wings, but you were not willing' (Matt. 23:37). The Lord Jesus is the LORD who guarantees protection and security to all who take refuge in him. All who do, experience his transforming kindness.

How the Lord uses apparently insignificant people as channels of his transforming kindness

Other histories of the time when the events of Ruth took place would probably overlook the lives of two destitute widows. But they were the Lord's chosen channels of his transforming kindness to his people. As they experienced the Lord's kindness, they were part of his plan to bring others to be transformed by his kindness. That is a pattern the Lord has followed throughout human history. It is a pattern he continues to follow today. As Paul writes to the church in Corinth:

Caught up in the chaos caused by everyone doing as he or she saw fit, her life, once full, had become bitter and empty. Having lost her husband and her sons, and with no apparent hope of grand-children, the future looked bleak.

> Brothers, think of what you were when you were called. Not
> many of you were wise by human standards; not many were

influential; not many were of noble birth. But God chose the foolish things of the world to shame the wise; God chose the weak things of the world to shame the strong. He chose the lowly things of this world and the despised things—and the things that are not—to nullify the things that are, so that no one may boast before him (1 Cor. 1:26-29).

FOR FURTHER STUDY

1. Considering the book of Ruth as a whole, what are the main truths it teaches about the Lord?

2. Read Judges 19 to 21. What were the consequences on society when 'everyone did as he saw fit'? How does this compare with what we see in our society today?

TO THINK ABOUT AND DISCUSS

1. Why is it important to see the place of the Book of Ruth in the unfolding drama of the whole Bible?

2. What does it mean in practice for us to take refuge under the Lord's wings?

3. 'The Lord does not do coincidences.' How should this truth help us in our daily lives? How can we use the implications of this truth to help and encourage others, perhaps those who are in difficult circumstances?

4. How does the very 'ordinariness' of the story of Ruth encourage us as we live our lives?

1 Forsaking the Lord and its consequences

(1:1-5) Please also read Judges 2:6-19 and Leviticus 26:3-20.

Judges 2:6-19 provides the context for understanding the opening verses of Ruth 1. 'In the days when the judges ruled' is shorthand for 'In the days when the Lord's people forsook the Lord, rebelled against his rule (each man doing as he saw fit), suffered the consequences and needed a rescuer.'

Judges 2:10-13 shows that the spiritual faithfulness of one generation cannot secure the faithfulness of the next. It is true for a family, for a local church, and for a nation. A following generation may be able to ride on the coat-tails of their ancestors for a while, but it will not be long before their true state is revealed. So it was in the days when the judges ruled.

Judges 2:14-15 sets out the consequences for the Lord's people of forsaking him. In his anger, God handed them over to raiders who plundered them. He sold them to their enemies all around them, whom they were no longer able to resist. Whenever they went out to fight, the hand of the Lord was against them to defeat them, just as he had sworn to them. They were in great distress. Judges 2:16 then sets out the role of the judges. They were deliverers raised up by the Lord, who saved the people out of the hands of these raiders.

Ruth 1:1-5 helps us to understand three significant truths about living in a world where the Lord and his rule are ignored:

The Lord's warning of punishment is no idle threat

'In the days when the judges ruled, *there was a famine in the land.*' This was no ordinary land. It was the land the Lord had promised to give Abraham (Gen. 12:7; 13:14-17). It was the land the Lord had promised to give his people, the descendants of Abraham, when he rescued them from slavery in Egypt (Exod. 3:8)—the land 'flowing with milk and honey'. It was the promised fruitful land where food was abundant and where the Lord's people could enjoy the good life the Lord had prepared for them.

So why was there a famine in the land? Why was there no food in the land that the Lord had promised would be full of abundant fruit? The answer is that the Lord's warning of punishment is no idle threat. Leviticus 26 contains one of the many warnings the Lord gave his rescued people as he prepared them for life in the Promised Land. There was the promise of blessing as they followed his decrees and were careful to obey his commands (vv. 3-13), including the promise of rain in season, and the ground producing its crops and the trees their fruit. However, there was also the warning of what would happen if they did not listen to the Lord and obey him. The Lord warned:

> But if you will not listen to me and carry out all these
> commands, and if you reject my decrees and abhor my laws
> and fail to carry out all my commands and so violate my
> covenant, then I will do this to you: I will bring upon you
> sudden terror, wasting diseases and fever that will destroy
> your sight and drain away your life. You will plant seed in
> vain, because your enemies will eat it. I will set my face
> against you so that you will be defeated by your enemies;
> those who hate you will rule over you, and you will flee even
> when no one is pursuing you. If after all this you will not listen
> to me, I will punish you for your sins seven times over. I will
> break down your stubborn pride and make the sky above you
> like iron and the ground beneath you like bronze. Your
> strength will be spent in vain, because your soil will not yield
> its crops, nor will the trees of the land yield their fruit (Lev.
> 26:14-20).

Therefore, when, in the days when the judges ruled, there
was a famine in the land, the Lord was acting in accordance
with the warning he had given—even in Bethlehem, which
means 'house of bread'. Bethlehem was a fertile place, a
place of plenty, where the normally abundant grain harvests
provided much to eat. It was a desirable place to live. But the
'house of bread' became the 'house of no bread', in
accordance with the Lord's warning.

The Lord never makes idle threats. His warnings are as
certain as his promises. We do not live in the Promised Land.
Our physical circumstances are not those of the people of

Israel. However, through his Word, the Lord warns us of punishment—punishment for all who forsake and ignore him. He warns us of the reality of his anger against sin in both the present and the future.

Famine is not the only way the Lord's punishment of the rebellious has been expressed throughout history. According to Romans 1:18-32 his wrath is being revealed in the present against all the godlessness and wickedness of men. As people exchange the truth of God for a lie and worship and serve created things rather than him, he gives them over to a depraved mind to do what ought not to be done. And he warns repeatedly of the future day of his wrath when his righteous judgement will be revealed and he will judge the world with justice by the man he has appointed (see Rom. 2:5 and Acts 17:31).

> The Lord never makes idle threats. His warnings are as certain as his promises.

Every warning God gives of judgement must be taken seriously, including those given to professing Christians. If we play with some secret sin we need to heed the warning of self-deception. 'Do not be deceived: God cannot be mocked. A man reaps what he sows. The one who sows to please his sinful nature, from that nature will reap destruction; the one who sows to please the Spirit, from the Spirit will reap eternal life' (Gal. 6:7-8). The Lord Jesus himself warns professing Christians, 'Not everyone who says to me, "Lord, Lord", will enter the kingdom of heaven, but only he who does the will of my Father who is in heaven. Many will say to me on that day, "Lord, Lord, did we not prophesy in your name, and in your name drive out demons and perform many miracles?" Then I will tell them plainly, "I never knew you. Away from me, you evildoers!"' (Matt. 7:21-23).

Understanding that the Lord's warnings of punishment are no idle threat gives a responsibility to share his warnings with others. God's warnings are an essential part of the gospel of our Lord Jesus Christ. Christians are called to be like watchmen on a city wall who warn inhabitants of the danger that is coming (see Ezek. 3:16-19). People need to know that God is right to be angry, that God is right to punish sin, and that the day of his wrath is coming. His warnings are themselves acts of kindness and patience, calling people to repentance. The Lord is slow to anger. His wrath does not come quickly. But it will come and those who believe his warnings must proclaim them.

Some may laugh at the suggestion that God will punish sin. Others, hearing his warnings, will think they apply to others, but not to them. The reaction of others must not stop those who take his warnings seriously from proclaiming them. Ruth 1:1 illustrates that the Lord's warnings of punishment are no idle threat.

Ignoring the Lord's rule is something to be taken seriously

Verses 1 and 2 move from telling us about the time and place of the story to telling us about a man and his family, who, because of the famine, went to live for a while in the country of Moab. The man's name was Elimelech. It was a great name for an Israelite. It means 'God is King' or 'God is my King'. It expressed the right attitude God's people should have— living in submission to God's rule. The tragedy of these verses, however, is that Elimelech did not live up to his name. Instead of submitting to God's rule, Elimelech, like the rest of his generation, did as he saw fit (Judg. 21:25).

Exact details are not provided, but it is a fair assumption that before the famine, Elimelech and his family had a pleasant life in Bethlehem. The name of Elimelech's wife, Naomi, means 'pleasant' (1:20). They had two sons, Mahlon and Kilion. They lived in a prosperous area. They belonged to the prominent tribe of Judah. But then the famine came. Perhaps the conversation between Elimelech and Naomi went something like this:

NAOMI: Elimelech, I'm not coping. The boys are always hungry. Their clothes are hanging off them and what I gave them for dinner today wouldn't feed a fly.

ELIMELECH: I know, dear. I'm doing my best, but nothing is growing. The ground is like bronze, and it is the same in everyone else's fields. The trees have no fruit.

NAOMI: Is there nothing we can do?

ELIMELECH: Naomi, I've been thinking. There is no end in sight. If this famine goes on much longer, we and the boys could die. I was wondering if we should pack up and move to Moab. I heard someone say that there is no famine there.

NAOMI: Moab? I'm sure my dad or grandad said something about Moab and the Moabites. What was it now? I think it was something about us, as Israelites, not having anything to do with them. I wish I could remember.

ELIMELECH: Don't worry about that, dear. It can't do any harm. It will only be for a little while. Just until the famine is over. We will pack up and go tomorrow. You'll see. It will be best for the whole family. The boys, you, me—we will be safe in Moab.

And so, they 'went to live for a while in the country of Moab' (v. 1).

> Elimelech's aim may have been to protect himself and his family from death, but he could not cheat death.

If Bethlehem was a great place for an Israelite to live, Moab was the opposite, or should have been. Moab was not a place to which any God-fearing Israelite would choose to go for a holiday, let alone take their family to live there. The Moabites were descended from Lot, after a sordid incident with his own daughter (see Gen. 19:30-38). The relationship between Moab and Israel had never been good. It was Balak, king of Moab, who hired Balaam to curse the Israelites (Num. 22-24). The women of Moab then seduced the Israelite men to indulge in sexual immorality and to worship their gods, causing the Lord's anger to burn against his people (Num. 25). It is no surprise, therefore, that as they entered the Promised Land, the people of Israel were commanded not to make a treaty of friendship with the Moabites (Deut. 23:3-6).

Whether Elimelech knew this we don't know, but he should have done. One of the Lord's commands as his people entered the Promised Land was that his law should be read to the people every seven years so that it would not be forgotten (Deut. 31:9-13). The record of Judges indicates that this command was disobeyed. Very soon generations grew up knowing nothing about the Lord and his word. When the Lord's word is ignored, the Lord and his rule are soon ignored and men, like Elimelech, do as they see fit, to the detriment of themselves and their families.

Elimelech may have intended to live in Moab only 'for a while', but 'they went to Moab and *lived there*' (v. 2)—or, as it could be translated, 'remained there' (ESV). And Elimelech and his boys remained there in more ways than one. The account of their residence in Moab is the story of a funeral, two weddings and two more funerals! Elimelech's aim may have been to protect himself and his family from death, but he could not cheat death. The boys' names, Mahlon and Kilion, may be significant. Mahlon means 'to be sick'. Kilion means 'failing' or 'pining'. They may have been particularly frail children. That may have been behind the decision to go to Moab. But Elimelech could not avoid the date of his own death or that of his sons—as no one can.

His death left his family in Moab, with the result that his sons married Moabite women, one named Orpah, and the other, Ruth. Given the past history with Moab and the way Moabite women had led Israelite men astray to worship other gods, this cannot have been a wise thing to do. Throughout Scripture the Lord's people are commanded repeatedly not to marry outside his people. Mahlon and Kilion would never have married Moabite women if Elimelech had not taken the family to Moab. The decisions taken by parents have repercussions for their children.

Then Mahlon and Kilion died too. It is reading too much into the text to suggest that their deaths and the death of their father were the Lord's judgement on them for going to

Moab and marrying Moabite women. There is no warrant for saying that. However, it is clear that the plan to leave the Promised Land in order to save their lives failed. (It is possible that the sons of Elimelech provide a picture of the state of the Lord's people at that time. Doing as they saw fit, they were sick, failing and in danger. The solution to the problems caused by sinful rebellion is never of human origin.)

> It is possible that the sons of Elimelech provide a picture of the state of the Lord's people at that time. Doing as they saw fit, they were sick, failing and in danger. The solution to the problems caused by sinful rebellion is never of human origin.

With Elimelech dead, the focus shifts to Naomi, his wife, and the sad consequences for her of their stay in Moab. Verse 3—'she was left with her two sons.' Verse 5—she 'was left without her two sons and her husband.' 'O Mrs Pleasant, what has happened to you? Your husband has gone. Your sons have gone. You are a lonely widow in a foreign land. What a bitter pill to swallow.' No wonder she says in verse 20, 'Don't call me Naomi [pleasant], call me Mara [bitter], because the Almighty has made my life very bitter.' Not that she had a bitter spirit, rather she had had bitter experiences. Naomi was discovering first-hand that ignoring the Lord's rule is something to be taken seriously. When we ignore the Lord's rule, thinking we know best, there may be short-term benefits and short-term happiness, but these will not last.

'Consider then and realize how evil and bitter it is for you when you forsake the LORD your God' (Jer. 2:19).

The name 'Christian' means someone who belongs to the Christ—to God's anointed King. Elimelech's failure should prompt us, as Christians, to ask whether we are living up to our name. We need to ask ourselves:

AM I SUBMITTING to the rule of Christ Jesus, or am I doing as I see fit?

WHEN TRIALS COME and I experience the consequences of living in a society which has forsaken God, what do I do? Do I try and devise my own escape plan, or do I seek the wise instructions of my King?

THE DECISIONS ELIMELECH MADE affected his wife and sons. When I make decisions that will affect those close to me, what criteria do I follow? Do I act in fear or faith?

Ignoring the Lord's rule is something to be taken seriously. It has bitter consequences both for those who ignore his rule and also for those, like Naomi, affected by the godless choices of others.

Tasting the Lord's bitter pill prepares the way for experiences of his kindness

We saw in the overview that the account of the Lord acting in transforming kindness to Naomi and Ruth is part of the unfolding story of his kindness to his people in the generations since. However, we may be wondering how the tragic story of the first five verses of chapter 1 fits with the Lord's kindness, especially given the way Naomi views her circumstances in the rest of chapter 1. She says, 'the LORD's hand has gone out against me' (v. 13); 'the Almighty has made my life very bitter' (v. 20); 'the LORD has brought me back empty. ... The LORD has afflicted me; the Almighty has brought misfortune upon me' (v. 21).

As Naomi considered her sad circumstances, she understood rightly that the Lord was in control. The bitter pill she was tasting was from him. But how does this fit with his transforming kindness? As we carefully trace the Lord's dealings with men and women in the Bible, we see how the different aspects of his character always fit together. This means that tasting his bitter pill is never inconsistent with his kindness. The opening verses of Ruth tell us that tasting the Lord's bitter pill can often be the necessary preparation for undeserving people to experience his kindness. This is seen throughout the Bible, especially when we read of famine. In the time of Joseph, the Lord used the famine to bring salvation to the sons of Jacob, even though they were undeserving. In the time of Elijah, the Lord used a famine to turn his people back to himself. In the parable of the prodigal son, a severe famine was part of the process by which the wayward son was brought to his senses and turned back to his father. The Lord can and does use bitter experiences to prepare the way for experiences of his undeserved kindness. This is the common experience of the Lord's people throughout history.

> Sing to the LORD, you saints of his;
>> praise his holy name.
> For his anger lasts only a moment,
>> but his favour lasts a lifetime;
> weeping may remain for a night,
>> but rejoicing comes in the morning (Ps. 30:4-5).

For Naomi, tasting the Lord's bitter pill was not the only experience she had of the Lord. It prepared the way for a wonderful experience of his kindness. A hint of hope is given in verse 6. News came to Moab that the Lord had come to the aid of his people by providing food for them.

It is similar news that brings hope today to those who have tasted bitter pills from the Lord. The good news of the Lord Jesus Christ, who was born in Bethlehem, is that he came to give aid to his people. This is how the people of Nain responded when the Lord Jesus went to their town: 'As he approached the town gate, a dead person was being carried out—the only son of his mother, and she was a widow. ... When the Lord saw her, his heart went out to her and he said, "Don't cry." Then he went up and touched the coffin, and those carrying it stood still. He said "Young man, I say to you, get up!" The dead man sat up and began to talk, and Jesus gave him back to his mother.' Not surprisingly, the people were filled with awe and praised God. '"A great prophet has appeared among us," they said. "God has come to help his people." This news about Jesus spread throughout Judea and the surrounding country' (Luke 7:11-17).

> As we carefully trace the Lord's dealings with men and women in the Bible, we see how the different aspects of his character always fit together. This means that tasting his bitter pill is never inconsistent with his kindness.

The people of Nain were right. The Lord Jesus is God who came to help his people. He came to provide the answer to death, by taking upon himself, on the cross, the punishment that forsaking God deserves. On the cross, he took upon himself the sorrow that ignoring God causes. On the cross, he chose to taste in the place of others the bitter cup of God's wrath, so that all who turn to him will never have to taste the bitter cup of eternal wrath themselves. As this good news spreads, hope is given to those with no hope.

FOR FURTHER STUDY

1. Read Deuteronomy 31:9-13. How does the failure to obey the command given there explain the situation in Ruth 1:1-5? What are the implications for Christian families and churches?

2. Read Romans 1:18-32. What marks of the wrath of God can we see our society today?

3. How do the truths of Ruth 1:1-5 point us to the redeeming work of our Lord Jesus Christ?

TO THINK ABOUT AND DISCUSS

1. Do you think we take the Lord's warnings seriously enough today? How can we help ourselves and one another in this?

2. Consider situations in which we are tempted to live as if the Lord is not King. In what circumstances are we tempted to make decisions based on fear not faith? What other factors guide our decision-making, instead of faith in the Lord?

3. What experiences have you had of bitter trials preparing the way for the Lord's kindness?

4. How can we best help a Christian friend who is tasting a bitter pill from the Lord?

2 Patterns of the Lord's kindness

(1:6-22)

Our sense of taste is sometimes helpful in describing experience. This is true in the English language; it is also true in Hebrew.

'Bitter' is the graphic word used by Naomi to describe her circumstances as she made the journey back from Moab to Bethlehem. Three times the word is used:

1:13—'No, my daughters, it is more *bitter* for me than for you, because the LORD's hand has gone out against me!'

1:20—'Don't call me Naomi [pleasant],' she told them, 'Call me *Mara* [*bitter*], because *the Almighty has made* my life very *bitter*.'

Naomi's circumstances make her use of this emotive word understandable. Ten years earlier her life had been full and pleasant. Happily married with two sons, when famine came to Bethlehem her husband acted to protect his family by moving to Moab. But then bitter tragedy struck in the form of bereavement. With the death of her husband and then her two sons, Naomi was left alone—a widow in a strange land.

Her only family were her two Moabite daughters-in-law. Sorrow, pain and a sense hopelessness are behind her description of her circumstances as 'bitter'. Her future looked bleak.

However, as we examine the way the story unfolds, we discover that her circumstances were not hopeless. In Naomi's bitter circumstances the Lord was at work preparing the way for his transforming kindness. Three patterns of the Lord's kind dealings with his people are seen:

News of the Lord's aid prompts a return to the Lord (vv. 6-7)

'When she heard ...' (v. 6). How Naomi heard in the days before telephone, e-mail, radio and television, we are not told, but good news has a way of spreading. The good news was that 'the LORD had come to the aid of his people by providing food for them'. The news was not that the weather had changed, that the sowing conditions were good, or that the crops were starting to grow. All those things may have been true, but instead the news conveyed the truth that the Lord had acted to end the famine. As we saw from Ruth 1:1, the famine was from the Lord—an act of judgement because of his people's rebellion against him. But in his wrath, the Lord remembers mercy. His anger lasts only a moment. The Lord, who commits himself to his undeserving people, now came to their aid.

It is this news that prompted Naomi to return 'home' from Moab (v. 6). The words 'home', 'return' and 'back' all emphasize that Moab could never have been 'home' for Naomi. The land of Judah in the Promised Land was her true home. Elimelech's decision to leave Judah had not been a good one. He and his family should have stuck out the famine, waiting for the Lord to come to their aid. But news of the Lord coming to the aid of his people prompted Naomi to return, just as the Lord intended. It was his plan that she would return to Judah, as part of his coming to the aid of his people in a far greater way than simply providing food for them. Through Naomi returning home, the Lord was putting in place the people who would establish the family line into which the Lord Jesus would be born.

> The seeds of backsliding are in the hearts of all believers. All Christians have the potential to wander.

The Christian message is the news that the same Lord who came to the aid of his people in Naomi's day has come to the aid of the world in the Lord Jesus Christ. When the tsunami devastated the coastlines surrounding the Indian Ocean in December 2004, the television news showed pictures of aircraft dropping down aid to remote, devastated areas. In this world, devastated by the bitter effects of human sin, God did not just drop an aid parcel, he came himself. As the Bread of Life, the Lord Jesus gave his life on the cross to give life to all who will return to him. He died, the righteous for the unrighteous, to bring us to God. The Lord Jesus is the living bread that came down from heaven to give his life for the life of the world.

Our first ancestors, Adam and Eve, lived with God in the place provided for them. It was home. It was the place where they enjoyed a close relationship with God. Through their rebellion against God, they forfeited their residence in that perfect place. This reality has been repeated in the lives of all their descendants (us) as we continue to ignore God and rebel against him. The good news is that the Lord Jesus has come to the aid of his people. The message of his cross is that there is a way back to God. It is as that message is made known that those who are far off are prompted to return to God.

'Those who are far off' includes backsliding believers. The seeds of backsliding are in the hearts of all believers. All Christians have the potential to wander. Like sunbathers floating on blow-up beds on the sea, careless Christians can suddenly discover that they have drifted far from their Lord. It happens when we do as we see fit, instead of doing what the Lord says is fitting. The record of Naomi's return proclaims the good news that backsliders can return to God. The same Lord who showed restoring kindness to his rebellious people, to individuals like David, Jonah and Peter, continues to show that same kindness to his wandering people today. As an old hymn urges:

> Let not conscience make you linger,
> nor of fitness fondly dream;
> All the fitness he requireth,
> Is to feel your need of him:
> This he gives you;
> 'Tis the Spirit's rising beam![1]

Faith in the Lord promotes faith in the Lord on the part of others (vv. 8-18)

As Naomi starts her journey home the narrator describes the moving interaction between her and her two Moabite daughters-in-law. The words 'wept', 'kissed' and 'clung to' express the emotion of the scene as Naomi urged her daughters-in-law to return to Moab, resulting in Orpah leaving and Ruth staying with her. An important principle in studying Old Testament narrative is not to read more into the text than is there. While observations could be made about human relationships, a close examination of what was said and done reveals that, despite her bitter experiences, Naomi was a woman who had faith in the Lord. Consider the evidence of her faith:

She was a woman of prayer

In verses 8 and 9 we have her first attempt to persuade Orpah and Ruth to return to Moab. Twice she prays—'May the LORD ...' (v. 8); 'May the LORD ...' (v. 9). Prayer to the Lord is the expression of faith in the Lord. Naomi believed that the Lord orders and controls events, otherwise there would have been no point in her praying.

She believed that any good thing is a gift of the Lord's kindness

This is revealed by the content of her prayer for her daughters-in-law (vv. 8-9). She recognized that, if they were to have new husbands, they would be a gift of the Lord's kindness.

She acted unselfishly towards others

Naomi's words in verses 11 to 13 are moving. She urged her daughters-in-law not to sacrifice their future for her. Her thoughts were for their welfare, not her own.

She had a balanced view of the Lord

Understanding the Lord's sovereignty in all things, she recognized that her bitter experiences were from him (v. 13). Behind this appears to be a recognition that when she and Elimelech moved to Moab, it had been a bad move. She understood that the Lord disciplines his people.

She had an attractive faith

If her faith had not been attractive, Ruth is unlikely to have clung to her (v. 14) and expressed her desire that Naomi's God be her God (v. 16). Her faith in the Lord promoted Ruth's faith in the Lord. We might think that the bitterness of Naomi's experience would have had the opposite effect, but no. Faith that clings to the Lord in the face of bitter experiences is faith that promotes faith.

Consider the faith that Naomi's faith promoted in Ruth:

Ruth's faith was determined faith

Three times Naomi urged Ruth to go back, until, realizing that Ruth was determined, she stopped urging her (v. 18).

Ruth's faith was wholehearted faith

She clung to Naomi (v. 14). The word 'clung' could be otherwise translated 'united' or 'cleaved'. Ruth attached herself to Naomi like a limpet might attach itself to a rock. And Ruth's action was explained by her words (vv. 16-17). They can be summarized like this:

Your journey = my journey
Your home = my home
Your people = my people
Your God = my God
Your future = my future

At the heart of her declaration was her commitment to Naomi's God. This was not just a commitment to Naomi. Orpah went back to her people and her gods (v. 15). Ruth left her gods behind and wholeheartedly embraced Naomi's God.

Ruth's faith was serious faith

Ruth saw herself as accountable to Naomi's God. 'May the LORD deal with me, be it ever so severely, if anything but death separates you and me' (v. 17). Since all she knew of the Lord must have come from Naomi, it must have included this sense of accountability to the Lord. She was learning what the Bible calls the fear of the Lord.

Faith in the Lord, especially in the face of bitter trials, is frequently used by the Lord to produce faith in others. Often when a believer is least aware of it, the Lord may be using his or her faith to promote faith in him. As a watching world observes a submissive faith in the Lord, it is prompted to ask believers to give a reason for the hope that they have. It is a mistake to think that we need to make the Lord more attractive to others by giving the impression that the life of faith is easy. Faith in the Lord often shines at its brightest and most attractive in the reality of bitter trials. The suffering believer who clings to the Lord in times of trial is more likely to promote faith in others than those who appear to have 'successful' and 'straightforward' lives.

> Faith in the Lord, especially in the face of bitter trials, is frequently used by the Lord to produce faith in others.

For the Christian, accounts of the faith of others during times of trial are often a great encouragement to persevering faith. The list in Hebrews 11 of those who lived by faith is given to encourage faith that endures. The study of Bible characters like Joseph, David, Jeremiah, Daniel and Paul, and how they exercised faith in the face of trial, spurs us on to do the same. Reading Christian biographies has a similar impact. It is also why sharing fellowship with those who are clinging to the Lord Jesus in times of trial can often be a great stimulus to confidence in God.

Emptiness from the Lord prepares the way for fullness from the Lord (vv. 19-22)

The arrival of Naomi back in Bethlehem caused a stir (v. 19). The exclamation of the women, 'Can this be Naomi?' indicates the change ten years had brought. Pain, sorrow, grief, regret, poverty and loneliness had taken their toll. Naomi had gone away prosperous and full, but returned empty (v. 21). Her husband, her sons and her prospects had all gone.

What is notable is Naomi's recognition that the Lord was in control of all that had happened—'Don't call me Naomi,' she told them. 'Call me Mara, because the Almighty has made my life very bitter. I went away full, but *the Lord has brought me back empty*. Why call me Naomi? *The Lord has afflicted me; the Almighty has brought misfortune upon me.*' The question her words raise is, how did she say these things? Did she say them bitterly? Some would suggest that she did. However, the evidence would suggest otherwise, especially given the attractiveness of her faith to Ruth. There is a difference between experiencing bitterness and being bitter.

> Backsliders will often have a similar experience. Backsliding often happens when life is filled with things other than the Lord Jesus and the affairs of his kingdom, choking the Word and making it unfruitful.

Hebrews 12:4-13 teaches that, in his love for his children, God uses hardships to discipline them. He does it for our good so that we may share in his holiness. 'No discipline seems pleasant at the time, but painful. Later on, however, it produces a harvest of righteousness and peace for those who have been trained by it' (Hebrews 12:11). Hebrews 12:15 then warns, 'See to it that no one misses the grace of God and that no bitter root grows up to cause trouble and defile many.' The way to avoid a bitter root is to recognize that the Lord's loving discipline is always an act of grace.

Naomi's use of the title 'the Almighty' in verses 20 and 21 is significant. It is a title used in Genesis at times when the Lord promises to bless abundantly beyond human imagining (e.g. Gen. 17:1; 28:3; 35:11). Little did Naomi know that, despite the emptiness she felt, the Almighty was preparing the way for her to experience the fullness of his blessing. The narrator of the story hints at this with the final words of the chapter. 'So Naomi returned from Moab accompanied by Ruth the Moabitess, her daughter-in-law, arriving in Bethlehem *as the barley harvest was beginning*' (v. 22). The place of famine was about to become the place of plenty. Although Naomi did not know it, the Almighty—who had sent the news that had prompted her return—was about to replace her emptiness with fullness.

For many, part of the process by which they are drawn to faith in the Lord Jesus is an awareness of the emptiness of life without God. This is often something God uses to prepare people for the discovery that the Lord Jesus came to give life to the full. Backsliders will often have a similar experience. Backsliding often happens when life is filled with things other than the Lord Jesus and the affairs of his kingdom, choking the Word and making it unfruitful. Sometimes the Lord has to bring the backslider to an awareness of the emptiness of such things, to prepare the way for a renewed experience of the fullness found only in the Lord Jesus.

Ruth 1:6-22 describes a journey. Our journey through life as Christians involves learning to trust the Lord's loving providence in life's changing scenes. We need to recognize that even the bitter experiences of life that leave us feeling empty are within his control and are designed for our good. John Berridge, an eighteenth-century Christian, wrote to a friend, 'Sitting comfortably on the beach is very sweet after a stormy voyage; but I fancy you will find it more difficult to walk closely with Jesus in a calm than in a storm, in easy circumstances than in difficult ones. A Christian never falls asleep in the fire or in the water, but grows drowsy in the sunshine.' [2]

Imagine a magazine interview with Naomi today, approximately 3000 years after the events of Ruth 1:

INTERVIEWER: Naomi, do you regret those bitter experiences you tasted? Are you angry with the Lord because of them?

NAOMI: No. I am not bitter. I have no regrets over the Lord's dealings with me. I regret my sin, but not what the Lord has done. I can see now that even those bitter experiences were part of his transforming kindness to me, as he used me in his great plan to show his transforming kindness to all believers in every age.

FOR FURTHER STUDY

1. How does the description of the Lord coming to the aid of his people (v. 6) help us understand the gospel of our Lord Jesus Christ?

2. Read Philippians 1:12-14. How does Paul's message to the Philippians in those verses fit with the impact Naomi's faith had on Ruth? What encouragement does that provide for us?

3. Read Hebrews 12:4-15. What truths about God do we need to apply during times of hardship?

TO THINK ABOUT AND DISCUSS

1. What are we tempted to think of God in difficult times? How can we train our minds to see all our circumstances in the light of the Lord's sovereignty? Think of difficult times you have been through in the past—can you now see ways in which God's hand was at work, although perhaps you couldn't see this at the time?

2. What is the best news we can give a friend who has backslidden?

3. What are some of the benefits of trials? (See e.g. 2 Cor. 1:3-11.)

3 An example of conversion

(1:14-18)

Ruth's actions and words in these verses provide an example of what is involved in a true Christian conversion.

Conversion involves decisive separation

There is something decisive and once for all about Ruth's words and actions. Her decision to go with Naomi meant a radical break with all she had known up to that point in her life. For Ruth, life could and would never be the same again. Her decision involved:

Separation from one kingdom for another

In going with Naomi, Ruth was renouncing her citizenship in Moab. She was saying, 'The people of Moab are no longer my people. I am separating myself from them. My people are now God's people. The kingdom I belong to is God's kingdom.' One of the purposes of Jesus' death on the cross was to separate for himself a people who are his very own. He died to rescue men and women from the kingdom of darkness and to bring them instead into his kingdom of light. When someone is converted, it always involves separation from the kingdom of sin into which we are born, for the Kingdom of Jesus into which we are brought by his death on the cross.

Separation from many gods for the one true God

In Moab, Ruth would have been a worshipper of the many gods of Moab. Going with Naomi, she was separating herself from those gods for the one true God—the Lord. The gospel of the Lord Jesus Christ calls us to turn to God from idols to serve the living and true God. It calls us to separate ourselves from all those things that are filling the Number One spot in our lives, which is rightfully God's.

Separation from those who remain as they are

For Ruth, her conversion meant separation from her sister-in-law, Orpah. Christian conversion will often separate us from our peers. A dividing line is crossed. We do not leave the world. We do not stop belonging to our human families, but we are no longer the same as others. Jesus taught that his gospel brings division between the converted and unconverted (see e.g. Matt. 10:34-39). The separation involved in conversion may be costly.

Conversion involves total identification

Ruth clung to Naomi. The word translated 'clung to' is the word used in Genesis 2:24 to describe what happens when a man and a woman are united in marriage. They cleave to each other—they are totally identified with each other. That is what Ruth's words in verses 16 and 17 reveal. From that moment her whole identity was bound up with the identity of Naomi. Conversion involves:

Identification with God and with God's people

Verses 16 and 17 are poetic in their structure. There are five pairs of clauses, as follows:

> Don't urge me to leave you
> or to turn back from you.
>> Where you go I will go,
>> and where you stay I will stay.
>>> *Your people will be my people*
>>> *and your God my God.*
>> Where you die I will die,
>> and there I will be buried.
> May the LORD deal with me, be it ever so severely,
> if anything but death separates you and me.

The structure reveals that the central pair of the clauses conveys the main point. At the heart of Ruth's identification with Naomi was her total identification with Naomi's God and Naomi's people. Ruth did not simply separate herself from the gods she had previously worshipped, she now identified herself fully with Naomi's God and Naomi's people.

To be a Christian is to be united to the Lord Jesus Christ, as by faith we cling to him. It means that his God becomes our God and his people become our people. Conversion automatically unites us to God's people.

Identification, wherever and whatever

That is the impact of Ruth's words—'Where you go I will go, and where you stay I will stay'(v. 16). Conversion covers every activity of life. No exclusion zones exist. Conversion involves saying to the Lord Jesus, 'I hand over my life to your control. You take the lead. You set the pace. You give the orders. I will follow.'

Identification, now and for ever

'Where you die I will die, and there I will be buried' (v. 17). Ruth's identification with Naomi was to be in life and in death. This identification is seen in Christian baptism. When a Christian is baptized it symbolizes total identification with the Lord Jesus Christ in his death and resurrection. Conversion involves an inseparable union between the Christian and the Lord Jesus.

Conversion involves single-minded determination

A determination not open to discussion

Ruth said, 'Don't urge me to leave you or to turn back from you' (v. 16). Jesus said, 'No one who puts his hand to the plough and looks back is fit for service in the kingdom of God' (Luke 9:62).

A determination before the Lord

'May the LORD deal with me, be it ever so severely, if anything but death separates you and me'(v. 17). It was a

> To be a Christian is to be united to the Lord Jesus Christ, as by faith we cling to him. It means that his God becomes our God and his people become our people. Conversion automatically unites us to God's people.

determination for which she considered herself accountable to the Lord. It was a commitment she meant to see through. Jesus calls for a similar single-minded determination. He says, 'If anyone would come after me, he must deny himself and take up his cross daily and follow me. For whoever wants to save his life will lose it, but whoever loses his life for me will save it' (Luke 9:23-24). Conversion is a one-way ticket; a one-way journey; an irrevocable commitment to the Lord Jesus, with no escape clause.

The seventeenth-century preacher John Wesley wrote the following prayer, summing up the impact of Christian conversion:

I am no longer my own but yours.
Put me to what you will,
rank me with whom you will;
put me to doing, put me to suffering;
let me be employed for you or laid aside for you,
exalted for you or brought low for you;
let me be full, let me be empty,
let me have all things, let me have nothing;
I freely and wholeheartedly yield all things to

your pleasure and disposal.

And now, glorious and blessed God,
Father, Son and Holy Spirit,
you are mine and I am yours. So be it.
And the covenant made on earth,
let it be ratified in heaven. Amen.[3]

For further study ▶

FOR FURTHER STUDY

1. Read Luke 9:57-62. How does the example of Ruth illustrate the teaching of our Lord Jesus about true discipleship?

2. Why is it impossible to separate identification with the Lord Jesus and identification with his people?

TO THINK ABOUT AND DISCUSS

1. What are some of the radical consequences of conversion faced by believers in society today? Why is it important not to hide these consequences as part of sharing the gospel?

2. What evidence of conversion would we expect to see in the life of someone who is genuinely converted? Should we expect new converts to show all this evidence immediately? How should we deal with someone who claims to be a Christian, yet whose life does not show this evidence?

4 What a difference a day can make!

(2:1-23) Please also read Deuteronomy 15:7-11 & 24:19-22

Ruth 2 should make us smile. But as Naomi and Ruth arrived in Bethlehem from Moab, they had little to smile about.

Widowed, destitute, poor, vulnerable, they had no option but to rely on the laws of Israel that allowed the alien and widow, the poor and disadvantaged, to pick up the leftovers after the harvesters had reaped the crops. Ruth's request 'Let me go to the fields and pick up the leftover grain behind anyone in whose eyes I find favour' (v. 2), was a wise suggestion. Naomi's answer, 'Go ahead, my daughter', has the sense of, 'You had better. It is the only option. Otherwise the cupboard will stay bare.'

But as we fast-forward to the end of the chapter, the situation has been transformed. Verses 2 to 22 cover one day. And at the end of that day we can sense the unexpected smile its events must have brought to Naomi and Ruth's faces. Having left with nothing in the morning, hoping that someone might show her favour, Ruth returned, not with a few leftovers, but weighed down with an abundance of barley! An ephah (v. 17) is 3/5ths of a bushel, 22 litres or 5 gallons. An ephah was also a large container big enough to hold a person. The value of an ephah of barley was about half a month's wages. Imagine Ruth's tired but contented smile as she staggered home with her load. Imagine what her mother-in-law *saw* (v. 18). Imagine the smile on Naomi's face as she asked, 'Where did you glean today? Where did you work? Blessed be the man who took notice of you!' (v. 19). Imagine the even bigger smile on Naomi's face as Ruth told her the identity of the man who had shown her such favour, resulting in the declaration about the Lord, 'he has not stopped showing his kindness to the living and the dead' (v. 20).

> The word 'favour' (v. 2) conveys the idea of kindness beyond what is due or usual. That was what Ruth and Naomi experienced that smile-producing day, and Naomi recognized it to be the lavish favour of the Lord himself.

The word 'favour' (v. 2) conveys the idea of kindness beyond what is due or usual. That was what Ruth and Naomi experienced that smile-producing day, and Naomi recognized it to be the lavish favour of the Lord himself. The Bible makes clear that, while in his righteousness the Lord does show anger in response to human arrogance and rebellion, he also delights to show favour and kindness. In particular, he delights to show lavish favour to those who take refuge in him (v. 12). When, ten years earlier, Elimelech and Naomi had left Bethlehem for Moab, doing what they thought was right, they were, in effect, removing themselves from the refuge of the wings of the God of Israel. Returning to Bethlehem, Naomi had returned to the shadow of his wings, where she and Ruth started to experience the favour he promises to those who take refuge there.

The description of that day of smile-producing kindness can be summarized under three headings:

The Lord's lavish favour is meticulously planned (vv. 1-4)

Under the direction of the Holy Spirit, the human author of Ruth provides an important piece of background information. 'Now Naomi had a relative on her husband's side from the clan of Elimelech, a man of standing, whose name was Boaz' (v. 1) Verses 2-3 then record the decision of Ruth to go off to the fields in the hope of picking up leftover grain behind 'anyone' in whose eyes she might find favour. Naomi agrees, without any direction as to where Ruth should go. 'So she went out and began to glean in the fields behind the harvesters' (v. 3). Ruth was a foreigner. It would seem that she knew nothing about whose field was whose, and that she knew nothing about Boaz and his relationship to Elimelech.

'As it turned out, she found herself working in a field belonging to Boaz, who was from the clan of Elimelech' (v. 3). The Authorized Version translates it '*her hap* was to light on a part of the field belonging unto Boaz, who was of the kindred of Elimelech.' We might say, 'As luck would have it.' But the Lord does not do luck! His work is never haphazard and scatty. He plans and pre-arranges. The field Ruth 'just so happened' to light upon was the very field the Lord had planned. There is a mystery here beyond our full comprehension. The Bible teaches that the Lord's sovereign plan incorporates the willing choices of men and women for which they are accountable. This is most clearly illustrated by the cross of the Lord Jesus Christ. As the early church prayed in Acts 4:27-28, 'Herod and Pontius Pilate met together with the Gentiles and the people of Israel in this city to conspire against your holy servant Jesus, whom you anointed. They did what your power and will had decided beforehand should happen.' Ruth chose to go to that particular field, but she was doing what the Lord in his power and will had decided beforehand should happen.

> There is a mystery here beyond our full comprehension. The Bible teaches that the Lord's sovereign plan incorporates the willing choices of men and women for which they are accountable.

This is reinforced by the start of verse 4, 'Just then Boaz arrived.' 'Just then', or 'Behold'. The idea is, 'Would you believe it!' Remember, the narrator has given us advance notice of the existence of Boaz. Now he turns up! And this is all designed to reveal that the Lord meticulously planned this apparent coincidence, which would result in an experience of his lavish favour. It was true then. It is true now. The Lord's plan to lavish favour on Ruth and Naomi was part of his even greater plan of lavishing favour upon men and women of future generations through our Lord Jesus Christ. No part of his meticulous plan was left to chance. Nothing the Lord ever does is down to luck. It was the Lord who, without her knowing it, caused Ruth to pick Boaz's field in which to seek favour in the eyes of 'someone'!

The Lord's lavish favour is channelled through 'Mr Right' (vv. 4-16)

The middle section of the chapter introduces us to Boaz. He is 'Mr Right', in the sense that he was the ideal man for the Lord to use as his channel of lavish favour to the women. His qualifications were as follows:

HE WAS A RELATIVE (V. 1)—the significance of this will become clear in Ruth 3. As a relative of Naomi he had responsibility to care for needy members of the family.

HE WAS A MAN OF STANDING (V. 1)—a man of resources able to meet the needs of the two women.

HE WAS GODLY (V. 4)—to refer to the Lord was the normal thing for Boaz to do, even in the way he conversed with his employees. With Boaz there was no gap between the spiritual and the material, the secular and the sacred. His men knew that the Lord was at the centre of his thinking. By implication he was a good employer who wanted his men to know the Lord was with them. It seems clear that Boaz had stayed in Bethlehem during the time of famine, while others, like Elimelech, left. Staying in the place the Lord had given, Boaz then experienced the Lord coming to the aid of his people.

HE WAS OBEDIENT (VV. 6-7)—obedient to the law of the Lord, which said, 'When you are harvesting in your field and you overlook a sheaf, do not go back to get it. Leave it for the alien, the fatherless and the widow, so that the LORD your God may bless you in all the work of your hands' (Deut. 24:19). Knowing their boss, Boaz's men knew that he would agree to an alien and widow like Ruth gleaning in his field. They had not chased her away.

HE WAS WELCOMING (VV. 8, 14)—hospitable to an alien. Not treating Ruth as a foreigner, Boaz called her 'My daughter', a warm term. Then, at mealtime, he invited her to eat with him, sharing his food with her.

HE WAS SENSITIVE (VV. 8-9)—considerate of Ruth's needs, he told her to stay with his servant girls.

HE PROVIDED FOR RUTH (VV. 9-10)—giving her protection, by telling his men not to touch her. He supplied refreshment, telling her she could drink from the water jars his men had filled.

HE WAS GENEROUS (VV. 14-16)—to the point of overload. When it came to lunchtime he asked Ruth to eat with him and his men. He shared bread and wine with her. She ate all she wanted and had some left over. Then Boaz gave instructions that exceeded what the law required, telling his men to pull out stalks for her to pick up (v. 16). No wonder she went home with so much.

Boaz was 'Mr Right' for Ruth and Naomi. He was ideally suited and perfectly prepared by the Lord to be the channel of his lavish kindness to them. As such he prefigured the 'Mr Right' through whom the Lord's lavish kindness comes to all who take refuge in him today. In John 5:39 the Lord Jesus said of the Old Testament Scriptures, 'These are the Scriptures that testify about me.' That includes Ruth 2. As Boaz is described we are given a description of the Lord Jesus, who came as the perfectly prepared and perfectly suited channel of the Lord's favour to sinners.

Consider the Lord Jesus:

HE LEFT HEAVEN and became our *relative*, as he took on human flesh.

AS THE GOD-MAN he was and is a man of standing, worthy and with all the resources of God at his disposal. In our destitute state, we need these resources.

IN HIS HUMANITY, he was the most godly man that has ever lived. With Jesus there was no division between the sacred and the secular, the spiritual and the material.

HE WAS OBEDIENT. In his humanity, he lived in perfect submission to the law of the Lord, in a way no one has before or since.

HE WAS WELCOMING of all who took refuge in him. Wherever they were from, whatever their background, he welcomed all who came to him. He was criticized for welcoming and eating with 'sinners'. The invitation to Ruth to have some bread and wine points us to the Last Supper, with the bread and wine providing a picture of the provision the Lord Jesus was going to make on the cross, and the welcome he extends to all who take refuge in him, to share table fellowship with him. It also points us forward to the feast in the eternal kingdom of heaven, which the Lord Jesus will share with his people.

HE WAS SENSITIVE, dealing with each person personally and graciously—the widow, the prostitute, the distraught parent, the tax collector, even his mother, as he hung dying on the cross.

THROUGH HIS DEATH ON THE CROSS, he provided protection from the wrath of God against sin for all who take refuge in him. He also provides them with refreshment of his indwelling Spirit.

AND HE WAS GENEROUS. The words 'she ate all she wanted

and had some left over' (v. 14) remind us of the satisfaction of the crowd at the feeding of the 5000 and the baskets left over (Matt. 14:20). There is nothing stingy about the generosity of the Lord Jesus.

The Lord's lavish favour is hope-giving for the future (vv. 17-23)

> What a difference a day can make! Evidence of the Lord's lavish favour on that one day gave Naomi renewed hope for the future that only hours earlier had looked bleak and dark.

The closing verses of the chapter show Naomi's recognition of the Lord's kindness as she heard Ruth's account of the day. She saw Ruth returning laden with barley: someone had been generous. 'Who?' 'Boaz.' 'The Lord bless him! Despite all the bitter things I have experienced, the Lord has not stopped showing kindness to me. And oh, I've just thought of something: Boaz is one of our kinsman-redeemers. A relative with a special, God-given, responsibility to help us.' As Ruth then told Naomi what Boaz said to her, we can imagine the cogs starting to whirr in Naomi's mind, perhaps not wanting to rush ahead, but wondering where this might lead. So she told Ruth to stay with Boaz's girls.

What a difference a day can make! Evidence of the Lord's lavish favour on that one day gave Naomi renewed hope for the future that only hours earlier had looked bleak and dark. What a difference a taste of the Lord's lavish favour makes! It did not change what was true about Naomi's circumstances. She remained a widow. She had still lost two sons. She continued to be poor and life was hard. But she had a hope-giving experience of the Lord's kindness, which gave her reason to believe that, while the Lord's anger lasts for a moment, his favour lasts for a lifetime. It cannot be wrong for us to imagine Naomi going to bed at the end of that day with a smile on her face.

Ruth 2 calls for three responses from us as Christians:

1. Take time to trace the Lord's meticulous plan to show us his lavish favour.

Fast-forwarding the story, the lavish favour shown to Naomi and Ruth resulted in Ruth marrying Boaz, and them having a child called Obed, who was the father of Jesse, the father of David, the royal ancestor of the Lord Jesus. It is never out of place to reflect on how through all the events of the Old Testament the Lord was meticulously following his plan to lavish favour upon rebellious human beings. The Old Testament is the record of the Lord bringing every detail into play at the right time and in the right place, until, at just the right time, Christ died, the righteous for the unrighteous, to bring us to God. The Christian should reflect not only, as it were, on that macro-plan, but also upon the Lord's micro-plan in relation to each individual who takes refuge in him and experiences his lavish favour. For every Christian there is a story of the Lord's meticulous plan, slotting people and events and meetings and so much more together—often in a way that is only seen in retrospect—as he brings his people to experience his lavish favour. This is not just the case when we first experience his favour. The Lord delights in continuing to shower his lavish favour on his people—often in ways that are far beyond all they can ask or even imagine, as they take refuge in him day by day.

2. Hear the call to follow in the favour-showing pattern of Boaz and the Lord Jesus.

In his godly generosity, Boaz prefigured the godly generosity of the Lord Jesus. As a follower of the Lord Jesus, every Christian is called to do the same. The Lord Jesus came to show his lavish favour so that his followers would then be channels of his favour to others. One of the distinctives of the people of Israel was that, in obeying God's law, they would provide for the poor, the disadvantaged, the widow, and the alien. God's promise was that those who obeyed him would never lose out (see Deut. 15:7-11). The showing of generous kindness towards others is something the Lord often chooses to use to bring others under the refuge of his wings.

3. Take courage for the future by considering the Lord's lavish favour in the past.

Nothing gives greater hope for the future than past experiences of the Lord's favour. As John Newton's hymn puts it:

> His love in time past
> Forbids me to think
> He'll leave me at last
> In trouble to sink;
> And can he have taught me
> To trust in his Name

And this far have brought me
To put me to shame? 4

The Lord's favour does not mean a trouble-free life. At the end of Ruth 2, Naomi and Ruth are still widows, poor and without much, but they were able to smile about the future because they had received evidence of the Lord's favour to them in their distress. How often the psalms tell a story of the Lord's favour to his people, despite their unfaithfulness to him, proclaiming the message, 'See what the Lord has done: it makes sense to take refuge in him!' As we take refuge under the Lord's wings we are called to live in the confidence that, God being for us, no one can be against us. We can live, confident that the same God who did not spare his own Son, but gave him up for us all, will graciously give us *all* things we need as we face the *all* things of life (see Rom. 8:28-32).

For further study ▶

1. What other biblical examples can you think of where the Lord's sovereign plan is shown to incorporate the willing choices of individuals? (See for example Gen. 50:15-21, but try to think of others.)

2. Why is the obedience of the Lord Jesus so important to the Christian faith?

3. Read Romans 8:28-32. Note the use of 'all things' in verses 28 and 32. What is the ultimate proof that the Lord will provide us with 'all things' in the 'all things' of life?

1. Take time to trace the circumstances and people the Lord has used to show you his lavish favour. How should this encourage you?

2. What are the practical implications likely to be as we follow the favour-showing pattern of Boaz and the Lord Jesus? In what practical ways can you be a channel of God's favour this week to your friends? Your family members? Your neighbours? Your work colleagues?

3. In what ways might we record past evidences of the Lord's favour and provision, as a prompt to continuing trust?

5 Active faith

(3:1-18)

Operation Market Garden was a military plan aimed at liberating the Netherlands from the Nazis during the Second World War. It was a complex, ambitious, costly plan, which took a long time to prepare. Its implementation involved a huge number of people, each playing their part at a particular point in the plan's outworking. Sadly it failed. It did not achieve its objective.

God has a plan. In aim it is not dissimilar to *Operation Market Garden*. His plan concerns the liberation, or to use the Bible word, the redemption of sinful men and women. We might call it *Operation Kindness*. It is a complex, ambitious, costly plan, prepared over thousands of years. Its implementation has and does involve a huge number of people each playing their part at a particular point in the plan's outworking. The difference with Operation Kindness, however, is that while

Operation Market Garden failed, *Operation Kindness* has succeeded and continues to succeed as men and women experience the redemption that God accomplished through the costly sacrifice of the Lord Jesus Christ on the cross—the central point of the plan.

The sequence of events in Ruth 3 was all part of God's Operation Kindness. Reading the events of this chapter for the first time, the details may seem quite foreign to us. We may wonder why the chapter records the details it does. If the big aim of the story is to show us Ruth's place in *Operation Kindness* as the mother of Obed, the grandfather of David, the ancestor of the Lord Jesus, why did God the Holy Spirit not guide the human author to miss out chapter 3 and go straight to the events of chapter 4? But God the Holy Spirit has caused the details of Ruth 3 to be recorded for us and would seem to have done so for this specific reason: to illustrate that, as God implements *Operation Kindness*, he uses the active faith of his people.

> The Bible is clear that God is sovereign. He is in control. He causes all things to happen. He says 'What I have said, that will I bring about; what I have planned, that will I do' (Isa. 46:11).

The Bible is clear that God is sovereign. He is in control. He causes all things to happen. He says 'What I have said, that will I bring about; what I have planned, that will I do' (Isa. 46:11). Unlike our plans, God's never fail. But the Bible also teaches with absolute certainty and great clarity that, in causing all things to happen, he does so in a way that upholds the ability of individuals to make willing responsible choices and actions. Exactly how God combines his control of all things and our willing responsible actions, the Bible does not explain, but it is full of examples of him doing just that. Ruth 3 provides three such examples, as Naomi, Ruth and Boaz each play their unique part at a particular point in the outworking of God's great plan.

God uses the active faith of his people as they take initiatives on the basis of his Word (vv. 1-4)

The chapter starts with Naomi taking the initiative. The barley and wheat harvests were drawing to an end. Naomi had a plan. The aim was to provide a home for Ruth in which she would be well provided for (v. 1). The target man was Boaz, who had already shown such great kindness to Naomi and Ruth, allowing Ruth to glean in his fields (v. 2). Naomi shared her plan with Ruth in great detail. She had done her research. She knew where Boaz would be, what he would be doing and when he would be doing it. She knew how to prepare Ruth for her part in the plan. On one level this may appear to be a piece of complex matchmaking—an example of an older woman helping a younger woman to get her man. The clue that tells us it was not is the description of Boaz in verse 2 as 'a kinsman of ours'. This explains the basis upon which Naomi acted. She acted in accordance with what God's law said about a kinsman, like Boaz, and the role of a kinsman in the preservation of the family name and the preservation of the family property.

In Old Testament times it was vital that a man's family

name should be preserved. If he died without an heir, steps were to be taken to make sure that he had an heir who would carry on the family name and inherit the family property. The law said that the widow of the dead man should marry one of her husband's relatives, with the first son of that union becoming the dead man's heir:

> If brothers are living together and one of them dies without a son, his widow must not marry outside the family. Her husband's brother shall take her and marry her and fulfil the duty of a brother-in-law to her. The first son she bears shall carry on the name of the dead brother so that his name will not be blotted out from Israel. However, if a man does not want to marry his brother's wife, she shall go to the elders at the town gate and say, 'My husband's brother refuses to carry on his brother's name in Israel. He will not fulfil the duty of a brother-in-law to me.' Then the elders of his town shall summon him and talk to him. If he persists in saying, 'I do not want to marry her', his brother's widow shall go up to him in the presence of the elders, take off one of his sandals, spit in his face and say, 'This is what is done to the man who will not build up his brother's family line.' That man's line shall be known in Israel as The Family of the Unsandalled (Deut. 25:5-10).

Also relevant are the provisions of God's law for what was to happen when an Israelite family fell on hard times and sold their land. In such circumstances, the nearest male relative, called the kinsman-redeemer, was to redeem—to buy back—the land for his poor relatives:

If one of your countrymen becomes poor and sells some of his property, his nearest relative is to come and redeem what his countryman has sold. If, however, a man has no one to redeem it for him but he himself prospers and acquires sufficient means to redeem it, he is to determine the value for the years since he sold it and refund the balance to the man to whom he sold it; he can then go back to his own property. But if he does not acquire the means to repay him, what he sold will remain in the possession of the buyer until the Year of Jubilee. It will be returned in the Jubilee, and he can then go back to his property (Lev. 25:25-28).

These provisions of the law provide the background to Naomi's actions in verses 1-4. Ruth 2:20 reveals that she knew something of the law about kinsman-redeemers, since she calls Boaz 'one of our kinsman-redeemers'. On the basis of what she knew of God's law, and the circumstances that God had brought about, she took the initiative.

> That night there was an opportunity. Naomi was exercising the logic of faith.

Her logic is revealed in these verses. Ruth was young. She needed a husband. Boaz was a kinsman who was favourably disposed to her. That night there was an opportunity. Naomi was exercising the logic of faith. Putting God's Word side by side with the circumstances God had brought about, she used her mind to determine a course of action in harmony with God's revealed will. It is a reminder that God has given us minds that are able to reason and think things through.

Naturally our minds are warped and bent, prone to think in ways that are contrary to God's ways. But as we experience his mercy and start to live by faith in the Lord Jesus, taking his Word into our lives, he transforms us by the renewing of our minds, so that we can test and approve what God's will is—his good, pleasing and perfect will (see Rom. 12:1-2).

The knowledge that God is sovereign and will fulfil all his plans should not keep us from taking action. On the contrary, it should result in us taking initiatives on the basis of what he tells us in his Word. Banks accept standing orders from customers, instructing that certain payments are to be made until instructions are given to the contrary. God's Word contains his unchanging standing orders—his standing instructions—for his people. As we read them, he calls us, with the enabling of the indwelling Holy Spirit, to apply them to the circumstances of our lives.

> The knowledge that God is sovereign and will fulfil all his plans should not keep us from taking action. On the contrary, it should result in us taking initiatives on the basis of what he tells us in his Word.

True faith takes initiatives on the basis of God's Word. Applying it to marriage, imagine a young Christian man who feels attracted to a young woman. They enjoy each other's company and get on well. As the relationship develops he asks himself, 'Is she the woman I should marry?' What should he do? He should put his circumstances up against God's Word. What does God's Word say? Is she a believer in the Lord Jesus? If she is, good. If she is not, then to propose marriage would not be an initiative of obedient faith. If she is a believer, he should ask, is the growing friendship with her a help or a hindrance to his walk with the Lord Jesus? If the answer is, a hindrance, then asking her to marry him is unlikely to be an initiative of faith. The Bible also says that a husband must love his wife as Christ loves the church. The young man must ask if the woman he is considering is someone he wants to love and serve in that way.

Naomi illustrates the logic of faith: how we should put our God-ordained circumstances up against the standing orders of his Word and take initiatives in accordance with his Word. It is the logic that should apply to all the decisions of life. God gives us responsibility to make decisions, delighting to use the faith initiatives of his people in the outworking of his good purpose.

God uses the active faith of his people as they ask for protection on the basis of his Word (vv. 5-9)

In verses 5 to 9 we see Ruth's humble submission to her mother-in-law. 'I will do whatever you say' (v. 5), and she did (v. 6). Ruth's humble submission as, unknowingly, she plays her part in the outworking of God's *Operation Kindness*, reminds us of the humble submission of the Lord Jesus as, knowingly, he played his part in the same great plan.

As we examine what happened at the threshing-floor that night, two preliminary observations need to be made about details that may raise questions. First, verse 7 does not say that Boaz was drunk. He was 'in good spirits'. The harvest was good. He had enjoyed a good meal. He was rejoicing in the Lord coming to his people's aid by providing them with food. The Bible does not criticize godly people for being happy. Elsewhere it warns of the danger of drinking too much alcohol, which can lead to the sin of drunkenness, but that is not the issue here. Verse 7 records the facts without comment.

Second, there is no suggestion that anything immoral or inappropriate happened between Boaz and Ruth. There is no hint of sexual impropriety. Boaz was an upright man and Ruth a woman of noble character (v. 11). God's Word is clear that his good gift of sex is to be enjoyed only between those who are married, after they are married. There is nothing here to suggest that Ruth and Boaz misused God's good gift.

> The word 'garment' is the same word translated 'wings' in 2:12. Having taken protection under the Lord's wings, she was now asking for protection from a man God had provided, who was qualified to give her the protection she needed.

What verse 9 shows is that this encounter in the middle of the night was all on the basis of God's Word. As Ruth asked Boaz for his protection she did what Naomi had told her to do (v. 4). She noted where Boaz was lying, went to the place where he was lying, uncovered his feet and lay down there (v. 7). There is nothing romantic about smelly feet! In the middle of the night something startled Boaz (v. 8). What? We are not told. Perhaps a spider ran across his nose. Perhaps his feet felt cold. He discovered a woman lying at his feet. 'Who are you?' was a reasonable question to ask (v. 9). Again, notice Ruth's humility in her reply: 'I am your *servant* Ruth.' Then notice her request. 'Spread the corner of your garment over me, since you are a kinsman-redeemer' (v. 9). It was a request for protection. The word 'garment' is the same word translated 'wings' in 2:12. Having taken protection under the Lord's wings, she was now asking for protection from a man God had provided, who was qualified to give her the protection she needed.

In this, Boaz is a type of the Lord Jesus Christ. He prefigures the Lord Jesus, the kinsman-redeemer God has provided for all who will humbly ask him to protect them. Ruth's humble request therefore illustrates what is involved in both becoming and being a Christian. Becoming a Christian involves humbly asking the Lord Jesus Christ for protection as the Redeemer who died on the cross. All need his protection—his protection from the condemnation sin deserves. Self-protection is impossible. Only through his redeeming sacrifice on the cross is protection from condemnation available for all who take refuge in him.

Living as a Christian also involves asking for his protection each day. To seek that protection is an act of humble reliance. Protection is needed against the raging desires of our sinful nature; against the lure of the pressures of this world; and from the schemes of the devil, who prowls around like a roaring lion looking for someone to devour. Recognizing these great dangers, we should be asking our Redeemer continually for protection. It is as we, his people, ask him for protection that the Lord Jesus implements his kindness plan in our lives and, through us, in the lives of others.

God uses the active faith of his people as they accept responsibility on the basis of his Word (vv. 10-18)

That is what Boaz did. It becomes clear that he was under no legal obligation to act. He was not the nearest relative (v. 12). There was a kinsman-redeemer nearer than him. 'The LORD bless you' (v. 10) indicates that Boaz recognized the Lord's hand in what was happening. What follows shows his willingness to accept responsibility. The words of verse 11 are words of commitment. 'And now, my daughter, don't be afraid. I will do for you all you ask.' There was the obstacle of the nearer relative to be overcome, but he committed himself to act on behalf of Ruth and Naomi. He accepted the responsibility of acting for their good, on the basis of God's Word. He promised to do so promptly (v. 13). He gave evidence of his commitment as he sent Ruth home with six measures of barley.

> In this Boaz again points us to the Lord Jesus. In his humanity, the Lord Jesus accepted responsibility on the basis of God's Word.

In this Boaz again points us to the Lord Jesus. In his humanity, the Lord Jesus accepted responsibility on the basis of God's Word. Even on the cross he demonstrated his obedience to God's law as he fulfilled his responsibility to his mother by arranging for her to be cared for by John (John 19:25-27). As he died on the cross he accepted responsibility for the sins of his people as he took their condemnation, so that they would be set free from condemnation.

The way Boaz accepted his God-given responsibility also sets a pattern for us to follow. Active faith means accepting the responsibilities God's Word sets out for us. This includes the responsibilities of parent to child, child to parent, husband to wife, and wife to husband. In our relationships with fellow-Christians we have a God-given responsibility to encourage and care for one another, to sympathize with and serve one another, to speak the truth in love to one another, and to teach and admonish one another. In our relationships with non-Christians we have a responsibility to live before them in a way that makes the gospel of the Lord Jesus attractive, taking opportunities that come to speak of him.

It is noteworthy that as Naomi, Ruth and Boaz all revealed their active faith in what God has said in his Word, they all acted with unselfish, generous, costly kindness. Naomi took the initiative for Ruth's benefit, not her own. Ruth submitted to Naomi and asked Boaz for protection for Naomi's benefit and for the sake of her deceased husband. Boaz committed himself to acting for Ruth and Naomi's benefit. Each of them therefore points us to the Lord Jesus and the greatest act of unselfish, costly, generous kindness—his redeeming death on the cross. It is as we continue in the pattern seen both in Ruth and most wonderfully in the Lord Jesus Christ, that God uses

> Each of them therefore points us to the Lord Jesus and the greatest act of unselfish, costly, generous kindness—his redeeming death on the cross.

our active unselfish faith in the continuing implementation
of his great *Operation Kindness*.

FOR FURTHER STUDY

1. Read Romans 12:1-2. What is involved in the renewing of our minds and the testing and approving of God's will?

2. Read Psalm 36, noting verse 7. What encouragements are given to take refuge in the shadow of the Lord's wings?

TO THINK ABOUT AND DISCUSS

1. Having considered how the logic of faith might apply to the question of marriage, consider how it might apply to other decisions we may face, e.g. applying for a job; buying a house; using our free time.

2. How does the Lord's Prayer (Matt. 6:9-13) confirm the importance of seeking God's daily protection? What does a failure to seek his protection reveal?

3. What will it mean for you to fulfil the God-given responsibilities in the relationships that make up your life? Think about your responsibilities to your family members; your friends, Christian and non-Christian; your work colleagues; your neighbours; other people in your church.

6 Redemption provided

(4:1-22)

God delights in providing redemption. 'Redemption' is a Bible word with a Bible meaning. It assumes a problem. It presupposes that people are trapped in trouble and need to be set free from it.

The classic Bible example of redemption is the Exodus, when God set the people of Israel free from Egypt. In Egypt they were slaves—oppressed, suffering and in misery. But God acted to redeem them by sending them a man, Moses, through whom he brought them out of slavery and eventually into the land he had prepared for them. God so delights in redeeming people and is so expert in it that he does not only provide one illustration of his redeeming work, he provides many, including the story of Ruth. His redeeming work in the lives of Naomi and Ruth comes to its climax in Ruth 4.

The Vincent Van Gogh Museum in Amsterdam displays many of the well-known masterpieces of the famous Dutch painter of the nineteenth century. In the basement of the museum there is a display of sketches Van Gogh did in advance of particular parts of his final masterpieces. So, for example, on the first page of one sketchpad, there is a pencil sketch of a human finger. On the next page there is a sketch of the same human finger, and on the next another, and on the next another, and so on. If we were able then to take that sketch and put it next to a finger of a character in one of Van Gogh's masterpieces, we would find it was an exact match. Van Gogh, the master expert painter, produced these sketches—brilliant in themselves—all sketched in preparation for the final full colour masterpieces.

Every story of redemption in the Old Testament is similar. While stories like the Exodus are brilliant acts of redemption in themselves, they are actually only (as it were) illustrative sketches *in advance of*, and *in preparation for*, the ultimate masterpiece of redemption, when God provided for the redemption of rebellious sinners through the Redeemer, Jesus, to set them free from the chaos and disaster caused by sin.

As we study the redemption story recorded in Ruth 4 we discover that the redemption provided through Boaz is an illustrative sketch just like this. Ruth 4 shows that:

Redemption is costly (vv. 1-11)

As we saw in Ruth 3, a kinsman-redeemer was a close relative of a family who was trapped in difficult circumstances. When the man of the family died without leaving a male heir, it was vital that the man's family name should be preserved. The law said that the widow of the dead man should marry her husband's closest male relative (the kinsman-redeemer), with the first son of that union becoming the dead man's heir. It was also the case that, if a man died without an heir, his land could be taken over by his nearest male relative. The details of how that worked out in practice are not completely clear, but that is the backdrop to what we read in 4:1-11.

As widows, Naomi and Ruth needed a kinsman-redeemer who would provide an heir to inherit the land of Naomi's deceased husband, Elimelech. Boaz was ideal, but, as he told Ruth at the threshing-floor (3:12), there was a kinsman-redeemer nearer than him. Boaz had committed himself to taking action the next morning and 4:1 describes him keeping his promise and taking steps to see if the nearer kinsman was willing to act. Boaz waited for the unnamed man to come along (another 'coincidence'?), and got him to sit down before he raised the issue with him. He started with the land, verses 3 and 4. It all seemed an attractive proposition and the unnamed nearer kinsman said he was willing to redeem the land, until Boaz informed him that if he took the land he would acquire Ruth too and the responsibility to provide an heir for Elimelech in accordance with the law. At this the kinsman-redeemer said, 'Then I

> Every time believers gather around the Lord's Table they remember the costly act of redemption accomplished by the Lord Jesus on the cross—of how he willingly bore the cost of the redemption of sinners.

cannot redeem it because I might endanger my own estate. You redeem it yourself. I cannot do it' (v. 6). The cost was too great for the nearer relative. It was a price he was unwilling to pay.

How different from Boaz. He was prepared to accept that cost, illustrating the way the redeemers provided by God accepted the cost of redemption:

WILLINGLY—Boaz had no hesitation in taking on this responsibility (3:18). His aim was to settle the matter that day (4:1).

PURPOSEFULLY—All Boaz's actions are very deliberate and thought-through. He did not leave anything to chance. He made sure everything was done properly.

FAITHFULLY—In all he did that day he was fulfilling his promise to Ruth the night before (3:13).

UNSELFISHLY—It was not for his own benefit (4:9-10). It was to maintain the name of the dead man with his property.

Every time believers gather around the Lord's Table they remember the costly act of redemption accomplished by the Lord Jesus on the cross—of how he willingly bore the cost of the redemption of sinners. With the Lord Jesus there was no sense of his arm being twisted—of him being reluctant, or doing something against his will. He willingly paid the redemption price with his own blood. As Peter writes, 'For you know that it was not with perishable things such as silver or gold that you were redeemed from the empty way of life handed down to you from your forefathers, but with the precious blood of Christ, a lamb without blemish or defect'

(1 Peter 1:18-19). The Lord Jesus paid the price purposefully. The Gospels reveal that the cross overshadowed his whole life. He set his face towards Jerusalem, travelling there with resolution and determination, arriving at just the right time—Passover time—that through his death he might pay the price necessary for the redemption of sinners. He performed that costly act faithfully. He died in accordance with God's promise that redemption would be provided. And he did so unselfishly—not for his own benefit, but for the benefit of those he died to redeem.

> And can it be that I should gain
> An interest in the Saviour's blood?
> Died he for me, who caused his pain?
> For me, who him, to death pursued?
> Amazing love! how can it be
> That thou, my God, shouldst die for me. 5

But how does his death on a cross 2000 years ago provide redemption for sinners today? The answer is found in the second point Ruth 4 teaches about redemption.

Redemption is a legal transaction (vv. 7-12)

The town gate was the place where legal business was transacted. Boaz deliberately gathered the elders as witnesses (v. 2). The narrator provides necessary background information when he explains that in earlier times in Israel, for the redemption and transfer of property to become final, one party took off his sandal and gave it to the other. This was the way of legalizing transactions (v. 7). So, if you saw a man walking down the road without a sandal on, you would know he had just sold some land and that it had all been done legally. Boaz also announced to the witnesses that all had been legally transacted (v. 9), and the witnesses confirmed it (v. 11). The significance is as follows.

For Boaz to redeem Naomi and Ruth:

The law had to be satisfied not bypassed

In his sovereignty, God could have made things much simpler. The story would have been much more straightforward had Boaz been the nearest kinsman. God does nothing without reason. Given its connection with the bigger plan of redemption, it would seem that the reason for this twist in the plot is to show that for redemption to take place the law must always be satisfied, not bypassed. That is certainly true when we think of the redemption God provided through the Lord Jesus.

> he Lord Jesus paid the price purposefully. The Gospels reveal that the cross overshadowed his whole life.

The Bible is clear that the whole of humanity is in a mess because of their sin. The law of God demands that sin and rebellion should and must be punished in accordance with God's justice. In his perfection and righteousness, God cannot overlook sin. The just and right demands of his law must be met, and that is exactly what happened as the Lord Jesus died on the cross. In his perfection he died to satisfy the just demands of God's law in the place of others. Through the cross, the law was not bypassed, it was satisfied. On the cross, a legal transaction took place. And it was the satisfaction of the demands of God's law that Jesus proclaimed from the cross as he said, 'It is finished' (John 19:30). This leads to the second point of significance pointed to by the actions of Boaz.

The completion of the transaction had to be announced and witnessed

> Then Boaz announced to the elders and all the people, 'Today you are witnesses that I have bought from Naomi all the property of Elimelech, Kilion and Mahlon. I have also acquired Ruth the Moabitess, Mahlon's widow, as my wife, in order to maintain the name of the dead with his property, so that his name will not disappear from among his family or from the town records. Today you are witnesses!' Then the elders and all those at the gate said, 'We are witnesses' (vv. 9-11).

When houses or cars are bought and sold documents are signed, witnessed and recorded in public registers for all to see. The nearer relative taking off his sandal and hobbling away was a public declaration that the deed was done. The words of the elders and other witnesses confirmed it had been done. As he cried, 'It is finished' (John 19:30), Jesus was announcing that by his death he had completed all the legalities necessary to redeem sinners. It was an act witnessed by many. The completion of Jesus' work of redemption was then announced by his resurrection from the dead— something that was also witnessed. And what we have in the New Testament is the testimony of the witnesses whose task was to say, 'Yes, redemption was accomplished. God's law was satisfied, not bypassed. We were there. We saw the evidence. It is certain.'

It is upon this announcement and the declaration of the witnesses of the resurrection of the Lord Jesus from the dead that the Christian relies. Eternal redemption is declared to be certain because God's law was satisfied. The justice of God for every sin of the believer—past, present, future—was satisfied by the Lord Jesus on the cross, once and for all time. That is the basis of all Christian assurance, well summed-up in the second verse of the hymn 'Before the throne of God above':

> When houses or cars are bought and sold documents are signed, witnessed and recorded in public registers for all to see. The nearer relative taking off his sandal and hobbling away was a public declaration that the deed was done.

When Satan tempts me to despair,
And tells me of the guilt within,
I look to heaven and see him there
Who made an end of all my sin.
Because the sinless Saviour died,
My sinful soul is counted free;
For God the Just is satisfied
To look on him, and pardon me,
To look on him, and pardon me.[6]

Redemption is transforming (vv. 11-22)

Redemption transforms people's lives.

The transformation of Ruth (vv. 11-12)

From the time Boaz redeemed her, Ruth had a new identity, a new position and a new status.

> Then the elders and all those at the gate said, 'We are witnesses. May the LORD make the woman who is coming into your home like Rachel and Leah, who together built up the house of Israel. May you have standing in Ephrathah and be famous in Bethlehem. Through the offspring the LORD gives you by this young woman, may your family be like that of Perez, whom Tamar bore to Judah.'

The justice of God for every sin of the believer—past, present, future—was satisfied by the Lord Jesus on the cross, once and for all time. That is the basis of all Christian assurance.

Up to this point, Ruth has been referred to as 'Ruth the Moabitess' (see e.g. 1:22; 2:6; 2:21), emphasizing that she was a foreigner. Now she was Ruth the wife of Boaz, soon to be the mother of Obed. She was now a redeemed person, with a special part to play in God's redemptive purposes. The hopes expressed by the words of the elders in verses 11 and 12 are significant. Rachel and Leah were the wives of Jacob, the mothers of the tribes of Israel.

Tamar, like Ruth, was a foreigner. The people of Bethlehem were descendants of her union with Judah. Ruth would be like Rachel, Leah and Tamar—significant in God's plan.

With the benefit of hindsight we know that these high hopes were not vain hopes. Obed was the father of Jesse, who had eight sons, the youngest of whom was David, from whom our Lord Jesus Christ was descended. The significance of both Tamar and Ruth is confirmed by their inclusion in the genealogy with which Matthew starts his Gospel.

Redemption transforms those who are redeemed. All new Christians discover that they have a new identity. They become part of the Bride of Christ. They discover that they are not their own because they have been 'bought with a price' (1 Cor. 6:19-20). Every believer becomes part of the family of Ruth and Boaz through the Lord Jesus, through whom God continues to fulfil his redemptive purposes in the world.

The transformation of Naomi (vv. 13-17)

The narrator wants us to know that the birth of a son to Boaz and Ruth was the Lord's doing—'the LORD enabled her to conceive, and she gave birth to a son' (v. 13). The surprise is that the focus then shifts from Ruth to Naomi as we are told what the women said to Naomi. Back in 1:19 the women spoke about Naomi, exclaiming, 'Can this be Naomi?' Now they praise the Lord for the transformation he has brought about. 'The women said to Naomi: "Praise be to the LORD, who this day has not left you without a kinsman-redeemer. May he become famous throughout Israel! He will renew your life and sustain you in your old age. For your daughter-in-law, who loves you and who is better to you than seven sons, has given him birth' (vv. 14-15).

> The story of Ruth started with rebellion—with a family going their own way instead of God's, suffering the bitter consequences. It ends with the renewal of Naomi's life—and with others rejoicing with her in the kindness God had shown her by providing her with the kinsman-redeemer she needed.

It should be noted that the women speak here not of Boaz, but of the child born as 'kinsman-redeemer', saying of him, 'he will renew your life and sustain you in your old age.' Redemption transforms by renewing life and giving hope for the future. When she first returned to Bethlehem from Moab, Naomi had no hope for the future. Through the Lord's kindness in providing her with a redeemer, her life was renewed and the child in her lap gave her hope for the future. All this points to Jesus. As the Redeemer, he renews the life of all he redeems and gives hope for the future.

The name Obed means 'servant'. Apart from his name we know little else about him, but he was born to be a servant of God's redemptive purposes. That is exactly what our Lord Jesus was. He was the servant of the Lord, who came not to be served, but to serve, and to give his life as a ransom for many (Mark 10:45). He calls all he redeems to follow his pattern of service.

The story of Ruth started with rebellion—with a family going their own way instead of God's, suffering the bitter consequences. It ends with the renewal of Naomi's life—and with others rejoicing with her in the kindness God had shown her by providing her with the kinsman-redeemer she needed. All her hope was now focused on the son that was born, just as the hope of the Christian is focused on the Son who was born to be the Redeemer.

For further study ▶

FOR FURTHER STUDY

1. Read Psalm 49:7-9. How is the impossibility described there solved in the Lord Jesus Christ? (See 1 Peter 1:18-19.)

2. Read Romans 3:21-31. How does this passage confirm that through the death of the Lord Jesus the law of God was satisfied, not bypassed? What should be our response?

3. Make a list of some of the ways the New Testament describes the new identity of a redeemed man or woman.

TO THINK ABOUT AND DISCUSS

1. How important is the redemptive work of the Lord Jesus on the cross when it comes to Christian assurance? How would you use these truths to counsel a friend who is unsure whether he or she is truly saved?

2. How does the Lord's assessment of human history differ from man's assessment of human history? How should Christians react to news of troubles and disasters taking place in the world?

3. How should being a servant of the Lord's purposes affect the way we conduct our lives? Does it mean we can sit back and wait for the Lord to carry out everything he has planned? Why not?

OPENING UP RUTH

Additional resources

David Atkinson, *The Message of Ruth*, The Bible Speaks Today Series, IVP, 1982

Arthur E. Cundall and Leon Morris, *Judges and Ruth*, Tyndale Old Testament Commentaries, IVP, 1968

Barry Webb, *Five Festal Garments: Christian Reflections on Song of Songs, Ruth, Lamentations, Ecclesiastes, and Esther*, IVP, 2001

Endnotes

1 Joseph Hart, 'Come ye sinners, poor and needy'

2 Quoted in J. C. Ryle, *Christian Leaders of the 18th Century*, Banner of Truth, 1978, p. 243

3 Taken from the Methodist Covenant Prayer, www.methodist.org.uk/index

4 John Newton, 'Begone Unbelief'

5 Charles Wesley, 'And can it be'

6 Charitie L Bancroft, 'Before the throne of God above'

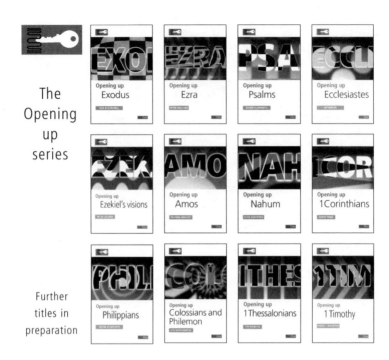
OPENING UP RUTH